CHOCOLATE KICKS

AND OTHER RECIPES FOR THE

CHOCOLATE ADDICT

BY Edna McHugh

PRICE / STERN / SLOAN
Publishers, Inc., Los Angeles

Second Printing — February, 1971
Copyright © 1970 by Edna McHugh
Published by Price/Stern/Sloan Publishers, Inc.
410 N. La Cienega Blvd., Los Angeles, California 90048
Printed in the United States of America.
All rights reserved.
Library of Congress Catalog Card No. 72-11002972
Standard Book Number 8431-0087

TO TRIS, WHO DIGS VANILLA

CONTENTS

PUDDING SCENE

CAKE-PUDDING SCENE

MISCELLANEOUS JAZZ

This is a book for the chocolate addict: for one who craves chocolate, whose body cries for it, who must have it or die. Don't worry. You are not alone. Help is here.

Help is here in the form of fifty ways to satisfy that need. Fifty beautiful concoctions (all containing chocolate) to bring joy and pleasure. If you're going to give in to your habit, swing with the best.

Try them all. Turn your friends on. Get your kicks!

COOKY
SCENE

CHOCOLATE KICKS

5 squares unsweetened chocolate
¼ pound butter
½ cup vegetable shortening
4 eggs
¼ teaspoon salt
2 cups sugar
1 tablespoon vanilla
1 cup sifted flour

Set·oven at 325°. Grease a 9" square pan.
Melt chocolate, butter and shortening
together over hot water. Mix thoroughly,
let cool slightly. Beat eggs with salt till
light. Add sugar gradually and beat till
creamy. Add chocolate mixture and vanilla.
Fold in well. Add flour all at once. Beat
till smooth. Bake for 50 minutes or till
done. Cut into small squares while hot.

*There's a recipe around for chocolate
brownies: a dry, pale brown thing that
really has no resemblance to this dark,
fudgy, moist delight.*

CHOCOLATE JOINTS

1st layer:

¼ pound butter
¼ cup sugar
¼ cup cocoa
1 teaspoon vanilla
1 egg, slightly beaten
2 cups finely crushed graham cracker crumbs
1 can (3½ oz.) cocoanut
¼ cup chopped nuts

Combine butter, sugar, cocoa and vanilla in double boiler. Cook over boiling water till blended. Carefully stir in egg and cook 3 minutes longer, stirring constantly. Stir in crumbs, cocoanut and nuts. Press into greased 9" square pan. Cool.

2nd layer:

¼ pound butter, softened
2 cups sifted powdered sugar
3 tablespoons milk
3 tablespoons instant vanilla pudding mix

Cream butter and sugar till light and fluffy. Beat in milk and pudding mix. Spread over first layer and let stand till firm.

3rd layer:

1 package (6 oz.) semi-sweet chocolate pieces

Melt chocolate in double boiler over hot water. Spread over second layer. Cool till firm. Cut into small squares. Serve chilled.

Eat them frozen. The hard chocolate top melts in your mouth MMM---MMM---MMM.

CHOCOLATE WEEDS

½ pound sweet cooking chocolate
1 tablespoon butter
2 eggs
¾ cup sugar
¼ cup sifted flour
¼ teaspoon baking powder
pinch salt
1 teaspoon vanilla
2 ounces pecans, finely chopped

Set oven at 350°. Grease 2 cooky sheets. Melt chocolate and butter together. Cool slightly. Beat eggs till foamy. Add sugar, two tablespoons at a time and beat till thick. Blend in chocolate. Add dry ingredients and blend. Stir in vanilla and nuts. Drop by teaspoonful on sheets, leaving room between for spreading. Bake for 12 to 15 minutes. Cool slightly before removing from pans. Makes about 4 dozen.

Here's a chocolate cooky that's really chocolate!

FUDGE STICKS

5 squares unsweetened chocolate
¼ pound butter
½ cup vegetable shortening
4 eggs
¼ teaspoon salt
2 cups sugar
1 tablespoon vanilla
1 cup sifted flour
1 cup chopped walnuts

Set oven at 325°. Grease an 8"x 16"x 1½"
pan. Melt chocolate, butter and shortening
together over hot water. Mix thoroughly,
let cool slightly. Beat eggs with salt till
light. Add sugar gradually and beat till
creamy. Add chocolate mixture and vanilla.
Fold in well. Add flour all at once. Beat
till smooth. Stir in half the nuts. Spread
evenly in pan. Sprinkle remaining nuts on
top. Bake for 35 minutes or till done. Cut
into sticks while hot, then cool in pan.
Makes 4 dozen.

If these don't turn you on, nothing will!

CHOCOLATE HIPPIES

3 squares unsweetened chocolate
¼ pound butter
2 eggs
¼ teaspoon salt
1 cup sugar
1 teaspoon vanilla
½ cup sifted flour
1 cup chopped nuts

Cheese Layer:

2 tablespoons butter, softened
¼ cup sugar
1 egg
1 cup cottage cheese
1 tablespoon cornstarch
½ teaspoon vanilla

Set oven at 350°. Grease an 8" square pan.
Melt chocolate and butter together over hot
water. Beat eggs with salt till light. Add
sugar gradually and beat till creamy. Mix in
chocolate mixture and vanilla. Add flour all
at once. Beat till smooth. Fold in nuts.

Cheese Layer:

Cream together butter and sugar. Beat in egg, cottage cheese, cornstarch and vanilla.

Spread half chocolate batter in bottom of pan. Pour cheese mixture over it. Drop remaining chocolate batter by spoonfuls over cheese mixture. With fork, partially blend into cheese mixture to marble. Bake for 1 hour or till done. Cut into squares while warm. Makes 25.

Eat them...they're hip.

CHOCOLATE WIGGIES

1¾ cups sugar
½ cup milk
¼ pound butter, softened
½ cup cocoa
½ cup chopped nuts
3 cups quick oats
1 teaspoon vanilla
½ teaspoon salt
½ cup cocoanut

Mix together and bring to a boil the sugar, milk, butter and cocoa. Boil for 1½ minutes. Remove from heat and add rest of ingredients. Drop by slightly rounded teaspoonfuls onto wax paper. Chill till firm. Makes about 3 dozen.

Flip yours.

CHOCOLATE GRASS

4 squares unsweetened chocolate
3 eggs, beaten
6 tablespoons soft butter
½ cup sugar
2 tablespoons flour
3 egg whites, beaten stiff
1 bar (4 oz.) sweet cooking chocolate
2½ tablespoons creme de cacao
almond paste, green coloring

Set oven at 350°. Grease 1½ " muffin tins.
Melt unsweetened chocolate over hot water.
Add butter, sugar and flour to beaten eggs
and mix well. Blend in melted chocolate.
Fold in beaten egg whites. Turn into muffin tins, filling each cup no more than two-
thirds full. Bake for 12 minutes. Remove
from oven and let stand 10 minutes. Remove
from tins and let cool completely on racks.

Melt sweet chocolate over hot water, blend
in creme de cacao. Spread over tops of
cakes. Color almond paste green. Form
into thin strips and decorate tops of cakes
with strips. Makes about 40.

*These adorable little cakes will make you
very happy.*

CHOCOLATE LSDs

4 squares unsweetened chocolate
1 can (15 oz.) sweetened condensed milk
¼ teaspoon salt
2 cans (4 oz. size) shredded cocoanut
2 cups chopped walnuts
1 teaspoon vanilla

Set oven at 350°. Grease 2 cooky sheets.
Combine chocolate, milk and salt in top of
double boiler and cook, stirring frequently
till chocolate is melted and mixture is thickened. Remove from heat. Add cocoanut,
nuts and vanilla, mix well. Drop by tablespoonfuls, 1 inch apart, on cooky sheets.
Bake for 12 minutes. Remove to rack, cool.
Makes 2 dozen.

*These will give you a good trip...the only
way to fly!!*

NOT VERY SQUARES

¼ pound butter, melted
1½ cups graham cracker crumbs
1 package (6 oz.) semi-sweet bits
1 package (6 oz.) butterscotch bits
1 box (3½ oz.) angel cocoanut flakes
1 cup chopped pecans
1 can (15 oz.) sweetened condensed milk

Set oven at 350°. Grease 9" square pan.
Mix butter and crumbs. Add all other ingredients and mix. Bake for 45 minutes. Cut
into squares.

Squares for the hip.

CAKE
SCENE

GROOVY CHOCOLATE CAKE

Cake:

4 squares unsweetened chocolate
¼ pound butter
1 cup hot water
2 cups sifted flour
2 cups sugar
¼ teaspoon salt
1 cup sour cream
1 teaspoon vanilla
1½ teaspoons baking soda
2 eggs, beaten

Frosting:

4 squares unsweetened chocolate
7 tablespoons milk
3 cups sifted powdered sugar
pinch of salt
1 teaspoon rum flavoring
1/3 stick of butter, melted
chocolate shot

Set oven at 350°. Grease a 13"x 9"x 2" pan.
Melt chocolate over hot water. Melt butter
in cup of hot water, bring to a boil. Mix
melted chocolate into butter and water.
Sift together flour, sugar, and salt. Pour
mixture into flour mixture all at once and
blend well. Add sour cream, vanilla and
baking soda and mix well.

Add eggs. Bake for 30 minutes or till done. When cake is almost done, start making frosting.

Melt chocolate over hot water. Mix milk with powdered sugar. Add salt and rum flavoring. Add melted chocolate and mix well. Add melted butter and mix some more. Spread on cake in the pan while still warm. Cover surface with chocolate shot.

A chocolate cake so groovy it defies description. Make it...eat it... you'll see.

SOLID CHOCOLATE

4 squares unsweetened chocolate
4 tablespoons strong coffee
¼ pound sweet butter, softened
½ cup sugar
3 eggs, separated
¼ cup finely chopped pecans
1 teaspoon vanilla
1/3 cup sifted flour
apricot jam (about 6 oz.)
chocolate glaze

Set oven at 350°. Grease and lightly flour
two 8" round cake pans. Melt chocolate
in the coffee over low heat, stirring constantly till chocolate is melted. Stir in the
butter, piece by piece, till melted. Remove
from fire and stir in the sugar. Pour into
large bowl, beat till blended and let cool.
Add the yolks, one at a time, beating after
each addition. Blend in the nuts and
vanilla. Add the flour all at once and mix
well. Beat the egg whites till stiff and fold
into mixture. Divide batter into the two
pans, spreading evenly. Bake for 20 minutes or until done. When cool, spread one
layer generously with jam and top with
other layer. Frost top and sides with
glaze. Serves 8.

Glaze:

1 package (6 oz.) semi-sweet chocolate bits
2 tablespoons butter
2 tablespoons light corn syrup
3 tablespoons milk

Combine chocolate bits and butter in the
top of double boiler over hot water. Melt,
stirring often. Stir in the corn syrup and
milk and beat till mixture is smooth. Spread
the glaze over the cake while still warm.

Solid chocolate through and through!

CRAZY CHOCOLATE CAKE

1 cup pitted dates
¾ teaspoon baking soda
¼ cup hot water
¼ pound butter, softened
1½ cups sugar
2 eggs
3 squares unsweetened chocolate, melted
    and cooled
1¾ cups sifted flour
½ teaspoon baking powder
½ teaspoon salt
¾ cup sour cream
2 teaspoons vanilla
½ cup chopped pecans

Set oven at 350°. Grease and flour a 13 x 9 x 2" pan. Cut dates into small pieces. Sprinkle with soda and pour hot water over them. Cream butter with sugar. Add eggs, one at a time, beating well after each addition. Add melted chocolate. Sift flour with baking powder and salt and add alternately with sour cream. Stir in the dates with their liquid and vanilla. Pour batter into pan and sprinkle top with nuts. Bake for 30 to 35 minutes or till done. Let rest in pan for 10 minutes, then turn out on rack and then onto another rack so that nuts are on top. Cool, then frost.

Frosting:

6 oz. package semi-sweet chocolate bits
2 tablespoons light corn syrup
1 tablespoon rum

Melt chocolate in corn syrup and rum in top of double boiler over hot water. Stir till smooth. Spread over top of cake. Cool thoroughly. Cut into 20 pieces.

Good things in this cake, but nothing as good as the chocolate itself.

STRAIGHT CHOCOLATE

4 eggs
4 bars (4 oz. size) sweet cooking chocolate
¼ pound sweet butter, softened
4 teaspoons sugar
4 teaspoons flour

Separate eggs, let whites warm to room
temperature. Set oven at 425°. Grease a
9 x 5 x 3" loaf pan, line with wax paper.
Melt chocolate over hot water, remove from
water, beat in butter with a spoon. With
electric mixer, beat whites till stiff, set
aside. Beat yolks till thick and lemon colored. Slowly add sugar, beating constantly.
Add flour, beat till just blended. Stir into
chocolate mixture, then fold into beaten
whites. Turn into pan. Turn oven down
to 350°. Bake for 55 minutes or till done.
Let cool completely in pan or rack. Refrigerate till well chilled, about 4 hours. Turn
out onto serving plate. Serves 10.

A French chocolate cake that says it all.

ACAPULCO GOLD CAKE

2 bars (¼ lb. size) German sweet chocolate
3 tablespoons water
3 tablespoons light cream
4½ cups sifted flour
4½ teaspoons baking powder
1½ teaspoons salt

¾ cup butter, softened	6 eggs
¾ cup shortening	1½ cups milk
2¼ cups sugar	1 tablespoon vanilla

Set oven at 350°. Grease, then flour bottom only
of 10" tube pan. Melt chocolate with water over
hot water, stirring occasionally, till smooth. Remove from heat and blend in cream. Sift together
flour, baking powder and salt. In large bowl, cream
butter with shortening till blended. Gradually add
sugar, continuing to beat till light and fluffy. Beat
in eggs, one at a time, beating after each addition.
Combine milk and vanilla. Add dry ingredients
alternating with milk, starting and ending with
dry ingredients. Turn about ¼ of the batter
into pan, then drizzle a layer of about 1/3 of
the melted chocolate mixture on top of the
batter. Repeat with two more alternating
layers of batter and chocolate mixture then top
with remaining batter. Bake for 80 minutes or
until done. Cool in pan for 15 minutes, then
remove from pan to rack and finish cooling.
Serves 20.

Those ripples of chocolate...like gold!

29

CHOCOLATE GO-GO-GO

Cake:

4 eggs, separated
5 tablespoons sugar
5 tablespoons sifted flour
granulated sugar

Set oven at 350°. Grease a baking sheet
well. Line with wax paper, grease again.
In small bowl beat egg yolks slightly. Add
flour and sugar and beat well. Gently fold
this mixture into stiffly beaten egg whites.
Spread mixture evenly in pan. Bake 17 minutes. Sprinkle generously with granulated
sugar. Loosen cake with spatula. Invert
onto wax paper. Remove paper. Roll up
cake. Refrigerate.

Filling:

6 squares semi-sweet chocolate
½ square unsweetened chocolate
3 tablespoons butter, softened
1 teaspoon vanilla
1 teaspoon rum
½ square semi-sweet chocolate, grated
    coarsely
powdered sugar

Over low heat melt semi-sweet and unsweetened chocolate, stirring with cold water till
dissolved and smooth. Remove from heat
and stir in soft butter, vanilla, and rum. Set
in bowl of ice. Stir until mixture is cold and
and slightly thickened. Unroll cake. Spread
with three-quarters of mixture, roll up.
Frost with rest. Sprinkle with grated chocolate, then powdered sugar.

You dig chocolate? Go!

CHOCOLATE BALL

Cake:

6 eggs, at room temperature, separated
1 cup sugar, sifted
1 teaspoon vanilla
1 cup sifted flour
pinch salt

Set oven at 350°. Grease and lightly flour two 1½ quart pyrex bowls. Beat yolks in large bowl with electric beater till lemon-colored. Gradually beat in two thirds of the sugar and beat well. Add vanilla. Sift flour with salt. Sift on surface of beaten yolks, all at once. Fold in. Beat whites with electric beater. Gradually beat in remaining sugar and beat till stiff. Fold into batter till no white spots show. Divide into two bowls and bake for 40 minutes or till done. Turn upside down on rack. When cooled, loosen with spatula and remove from bowls. With sharp knife, hollow out center of each cake leaving a 1" shell on sides and bottom.

Filling:

4 tablespoons butter
6 tablespoons flour
4 tablespoons sugar
2 cups milk
2 egg yolks, slightly beaten
1 package (6 oz.) semi-sweet chocolate bits

In heavy saucepan, melt butter. Blend in flour and sugar. Gradually stir in milk. Cook, stirring constantly, till smooth and thick. Add some of the mixture to yolks, stirring briskly, then return to milk mixture with chocolate bits and stir over low heat till thick and chocolate is melted. Fill shells with mixture and chill several hours or overnight. Place one cake over the other to form a sphere.

Frosting:

1 cup heavy cream
2 tablespoons sugar
2 tablespoons cocoa
½ teaspoon vanilla

Mix all ingredients, but don't whip. Chill for an hour. Beat. Frost ball. Serves 8.

Need I say it? Have a ball.

CHOCOLATE FLIGHT

1 package (10" tube size) angel-food mix
1 package (6 oz.) semi-sweet chocolate bits
8 squares unsweetened chocolate
¾ pound butter, softened
2 cups sifted powdered sugar
3 egg yolks

Set oven at 350°. Prepare cake mix as directed. Bake in four 8" ungreased layer-cake pans, lined with wax paper for 25 to 30 minutes. Cool layers, upside down, on cake racks. Remove from pans. Place one on top of other. Wrap in wax paper and refrigerate for 2 to 3 days.

Melt chocolate bits and unsweetened chocolate over hot water, cool well. Split each cake layer in two, making 8 layers. Beat butter with electric mixer till fluffy. Add sugar gradually, then yolks, one at a time, beating till very fluffy. Beat in melted chocolate till blended. Set aside best layer for top. Spread frosting between all layers and on top. Sprinkle with chopped toasted almonds if desired. Refrigerate for 1 to 2 days.

Take off!

PIE
SCENE

CHOCOLATE FLASH

Crust:

1 2/3 cups chocolate wafers, crushed
¼ cup melted butter

Set oven at 375°. Blend butter with chocolate wafer crumbs. Pour mixture into 10" pie plate and press crumbs firmly to bottom and sides. Bake for 8 minutes. Chill.

Filling:

2 packages chocolate pudding mix
4 squares unsweetened chocolate, grated
1 quart cream
chopped nuts

Make pudding as directed with cream instead of milk, adding grated chocolate to pudding mix. Chill, with sheet of wax paper directly on surface. Pour into chilled crust. Sprinkle top with chopped nuts.

A chocolate pie that tastes like chocolate. You'll feel the taste get to you.

CHOCOLATE HASH

2 cups vanilla cooky crumbs, finely crushed
1/3 cup butter, melted
1 cup heavy cream
3 tablespoons cocoa
2 teaspoons sugar
12 ounces semi-sweet chocolate
2 packages (8 oz. size) cream cheese, softened
½ cup strong coffee
pinch of salt
1 teaspoon vanilla
4 eggs, separated
2/3 cup sugar
chopped nuts

Stir butter into cooky crumbs and press into bottom and sides of well-greased spring-form pan. Chill. Mix cocoa and 2 teaspoons sugar into cream but don't whip, chill. Set oven at 350°. Melt chocolate in double boiler over hot water. Add coffee gradually to cream cheese, and beat till smooth. Add salt and vanilla. Mix into melted chocolate and stir till smooth. Remove from heat and cool for five minutes, stirring occasionally. Beat yolks with half of sugar till thick and lemon-colored. Slowly add chocolate mixture to yolks. Beat whites with remaining sugar till stiff. Fold into the batter and pour into chilled shell. Bake for 1 hour or till set. Turn off heat, open oven

door, and let cake cool in oven. Chill.
Remove sides of pan. Whip cream till stiff
and spread over top. Sprinkle with nuts.

A lot of good stuff put together.

COOL CHOCOLATE

1 package (8¼ oz.) chocolate wafers
¼ pound butter, melted
½ teaspoon vanilla
4 ounces semi-sweet chocolate, melted
1½ quarts chocolate ice cream,
      slightly softened

Whir wafers, a few at a time, in blender to make crumbs. Mix with melted butter and vanilla. Press a little over half the crumbs evenly over bottom and sides of 10" pie pan. Chill in freezer till firm. Turn ice cream into large bowl and beat with electric beater at medium speed till smooth. Gradually add melted chocolate (chocolate will harden and form fine pieces). Pour into crumb crust and freeze till firm. Pat remaining crumbs over top. Freeze till half hour before serving. Serves 10 to 12.

Black is beautiful!

SOUL CHOCOLATE

Crust:

2 cups chocolate wafers, crushed
1/3 cup melted butter

Mix and press into bottom and sides of 8"
square pan. Bake at 375° for 8 minutes.
Chill.

Mousse:

1 cup milk
2 squares unsweetened chocolate
pinch of salt
½ pound (about 32) marshmallows
1 egg yolk, slightly beaten
1 teaspoon vanilla
1 cup heavy cream, whipped

Heat milk, chocolate, salt and marshmallows
over low heat, stirring constantly till chocolate and marshmallows melt. Stir small
amount into egg yolk, mixing constantly,
then return to hot mixture. Cook and stir
over low heat one minute. Add vanilla.
Chill till partially set, stirring occasionally.
Fold in whipped cream. Pour into crust
and freeze till firm.

Food for the soul.

WAY OUT PIE

¼ pound butter, softened
1 cup sugar
1 teaspoon vanilla
2 eggs, separated
2½ squares unsweetened chocolate, melted
1/3 cup sifted flour
pinch salt

Set oven at 350°. Grease a 9" pie pan.
Cream butter and sugar till light. Add vanilla
and blend. Add egg yolks, one at a time,
beating well after each. Mix in melted chocolate. Add flour and mix well. Beat egg
whites with salt till stiff and fold them into
chocolate mixture. Bake for 45 minutes or
till pie is puffed on top.

*You can't get more chocolaty or more way
out than this!*

CHOCOLATE JUNK

1 cup heavy cream
2 tablespoons cocoa
3 tablespoons sugar
½ teaspoon vanilla
20 double thin saltines
1¼ teaspoons baking powder
4 egg whites
1¼ cups sugar
1 teaspoon vanilla
1 cup chopped pecans
chocolate shot or shavings

Mix together cream, cocoa, sugar and ½ teaspoon vanilla, but do not whip. Chill for an hour. Set oven at 350°. Grease a 9" pie pan. Whir crackers, a few at a time, in blender to make fine crumbs. Mix in baking powder and set aside. Beat whites till stiff, but not dry. Gradually add sugar, a little at a time, beating till stiff. Gently fold in vanilla, nuts and crumbs, mixing well. Pour into pan and bake for 30 minutes or till golden brown and firm. Let cool. Beat chilled cream and spread on completely cooled cake. Cover entire surface with chocolate shot or shavings. Serves 8.

Nobody can ever tell what it's made of. You can get hooked on this one.

CHOCOLATE BAG

4 ounces unsweetened chocolate
½ pound butter
4 eggs
2 cups sugar
2 teaspoons vanilla
1 cup sifted flour
pinch salt
1 cup chopped walnuts
1½ quarts ice cream
½ square unsweetened chocolate
1 package (10 oz.) frozen raspberries, thawed

Set oven at 325°. Grease two 9" pie pans. Melt
chocolate and butter over hot water, set aside.
Beat eggs till thick and lemon colored and gradually beat in sugar, beating with electric blender
till thick. Beat in vanilla. Mix in the melted
chocolate and butter. Mix in the flour and
salt till just blended. Fold in nuts. Turn into
pie pans and bake for 35 to 40 minutes or till
done. Let cool. Form ice cream balls on cooky
sheet. Make curls with vegetable peeler out of
½ square of room-temperature chocolate and
decorate ice cream balls, cover and freeze. Before serving, let pies thaw at room temperature.
Puree raspberries and syrup in blender, then
push through strainer to remove seeds, pour into pitcher and chill. Top pies with ice cream
balls, pour syrup over them. Serves 16.

This is my bag, your bag, everybody's bag.

PUDDING
SCENE

CHOCOLATE POT

2 cups heavy cream
2 cups milk
1 cup sugar
5 eggs
5 egg yolks
4 ounces sweet chocolate, melted
5 squares unsweetened chocolate, melted
1 tablespoon vanilla

Heat cream, milk, and half of sugar till skin starts to form. Beat eggs and yolks lightly with remaining sugar. Stir cream into eggs. Add chocolate, then vanilla. Let mixture stand for 15 minutes. Set oven at 350°. Skim foam off top carefully. Spoon into 12 pots or custard cups. Put them into deep pan and fill the pan halfway up with boiling water. Cover loosely with foil. Cook for 45 minutes. Remove the foil and cook for 15 minutes more. Cool, then chill thoroughly. Garnish with whipped cream if desired. Serves 12.

The true chocolate addict can eat all twelve of these!

CHOCOLATE SPEED

½ pound sweet chocolate
1 square unsweetened chocolate
4 eggs, separated
4 tablespoons sugar
4 tablespoons milk
1 pint heavy cream
1 teaspoon vanilla

Melt chocolate in top of double boiler. Beat
egg yolks, add sugar gradually, beat. Add
yolks and milk to melted chocolate and
stir till smooth. Pour into bowl and cool.
Beat egg whites till stiff and fold into
chocolate mixture. Whip cream and fold
into mixture with vanilla. Pour into 2 quart
soufflé dish. Chill thoroughly. Sprinkle top
with sifted cocoa. Serves 6 to 8.

*A mousse like this will give you energy for a
whole day!*

CHOCOLATE FIX

6 tablespoons butter
4 squares unsweetened chocolate
½ cup sifted flour
2 cups milk
1 1/3 cups sugar
6 eggs, separated
¼ teaspoon salt
2 teaspoons vanilla

Melt butter with chocolate over low heat.
Blend in flour and salt. Add milk and half
the sugar. Cook, stirring, for about 20 minutes or till thickened. Blend in beaten egg
yolks and vanilla. Refrigerate till needed
(this may be done early in the day.) Set
oven at 425°. Reheat chocolate mixture
over boiling water, stirring. Remove from
heat. Beat egg whites till they stand in
moist, drooping peaks. Add the rest of
sugar gradually and beat till stiff. Fold
into chocolate mixture. Pour into soufflé
dish. Set in shallow pan of hot water.
Bake for about 45 minutes, or till done.
Serve with softened vanilla ice cream or
whipped cream. Serves 6 to 8.

*Hot rich chocolate covered with masses of
cold sweet cream...you'll crave it.*

CHOCOLATE ALOT

8 squares semi-sweet chocolate
1 cup cream
1 package gelatin
¼ cup water
4 eggs
1/3 cup sugar
2 teaspoons instant coffee
1 tablespoon cognac

Melt chocolate in cream over hot water. Stir
till smooth. Soften gelatin in water. Stir
into chocolate mixture till completely dissolved. Remove from hot water. Beat eggs
slightly with sugar in saucepan. Stir over
low heat, stirring continually till warm.
Remove from heat, pour into large bowl
and beat till cool. Add coffee and cognac
to chocolate mixture, then add eggs and
fold in well. Pour into 1 quart mold rinsed in
cold water and chill till firm. Serves 6.

Chocolate Jell-O for the addict.

CHOCOLATE CRYSTAL

1 pound semi-sweet chocolate
6 eggs, separated
½ pint heavy cream
1 tablespoon liquor (rum, bourbon, or
    sherry)
chopped nuts
whipped cream

Melt chocolate over hot water. Remove from heat. Beat in egg yolks one at a time. Stir cream in slowly. Add liquor very slowly, stirring constantly. Fold in stiffly beaten whites. Pour into shallow serving dish. Sprinkle nuts on top. Chill thoroughly. Serve with flavored whipped cream. Serves 8 to 10.

It's too good for kids.

CHOCOLATE SWINGER

1 pound sweet chocolate, cut up
2 squares unsweetened chocolate, cut up
7 tablespoons strong coffee
2 tablespoons rum
5 eggs, separated
4 tablespoons butter
1 cup heavy cream, whipped
16 ladyfingers, split
whipped cream

Put all chocolate and coffee in a heavy pan over a low flame. Stir until the chocolate is dissolved, then add rum. Remove from fire. Add the egg yolks, one at a time, then the butter, bit by bit. Fold in stiffly beaten egg whites, then whipped cream. Lightly butter the 2 quart soufflé dish and line bottom and sides with ladyfingers. Fill with mousse and chill overnight. Serve with whipped cream.

Swing with this one, lovely mousse-type dessert.

CHOCOLATE COP OUT

4 eggs
½ cup sugar
1 teaspoon vanilla
1 large can evaporated milk (1 2/3 cups)
3 squares unsweetened chocolate
pinch salt

Set oven at 325°. Beat eggs with salt. Stir in half the sugar and the vanilla. Pour the milk into large measuring cup and fill with water till the amount reaches 2¼ cups. Cook the milk, chocolate and rest of sugar together till completely dissolved and well blended (use egg beater to completely dissolve.) Add this mixture to eggs. Mix thoroughly. Pour into 2 quart baking dish and place it in a pan of hot water. Bake for about an hour or till knife inserted in center comes out clean. Chill. Sprinkle sifted cocoa on top.

I wouldn't tell anyone it was custard, would you?

CHOCOLATE OUT OF SIGHT

8 squares unsweetened chocolate
5 tablespoons strong coffee
2 teaspoons dark rum
¼ pound butter, softened
½ cup sugar
4 eggs, separated
1 teaspoon vanilla
1 cup cream, whipped

Melt chocolate with coffee and rum in double
boiler over hot water. Beat in butter.
Remove from heat and beat in sugar and
egg yolks, one at a time. Let mixture cool.
Beat egg whites till stiff and fold into mixture. Stir in vanilla. Pour into a greased
1-quart mold, cover. Set in pot with about
2 inches of hot water in bottom. Cover
pot tightly and bring to a boil. Turn down
heat to simmer and steam pudding for 30
minutes. Cool, then chill. Turn out on
serving plate and decorate top and sides
with cream which has been sweetened and
flavored to taste. Serves 6.

Keep your eye on this one.

CAKE-PUDDING
SCENE

CHOCOLATE BLAST

4 eggs
¼ cup sugar
8 squares semi-sweet chocolate
¼ pound butter, softened
macaroons
whipped cream

Beat eggs with sugar. Melt chocolate over hot water and stir into egg mixture. Beat in butter. Line a 9" square pan with wax paper. Place a layer of cookies all over the bottom. Spread half the chocolate mixture on top of them. Repeat with another layer of cookies, then the remaining chocolate mixture on top. Chill for several hours. Remove from pan and serve with whipped cream.

Have a blast...you've got it coming.

CLOUD 9

1 (1 lb. 7 oz.) angel food cake
6 tablespoons rum
5 packages (6 oz. size) semi-sweet chocolate
    bits
6 eggs
2 teaspoons vanilla
pinch salt
1½ pints heavy cream
3 ounces slivered almonds, toasted in butter
    till browned

Cut crust from cake. Tear cake into pieces.
Sprinkle with rum, toss lightly. Melt chocolate over hot water. Transfer to bowl and
beat in eggs, one at a time, with electric
beater at medium speed. Beat in vanilla
and salt. Whip 1 pint of cream, fold into
chocolate mixture. Layer cake and chocolate into greased 10" tube pan, beginning
and ending with cake. Freeze for a couple
of hours or till firm. Run sharp knife
around side of pan and then carefully
turn out onto serving plate. Whip remaining cream, and frost top and sides with it.
Stand almonds on ends all over top and
sides of cake. Freeze till 30 minutes
before serving. Serves 18.

Drift away on this!

BOSS CHOCOLATE

¼ cup sifted flour
½ teaspoon salt
5 tablespoons cocoa
1 cup powdered sugar
5 eggs, separated
1 teaspoon vanilla
about 1¼ quarts ice cream, slightly softened

Set oven at 400°. Line greased sheet pan with wax paper. Sift flour, salt, cocoa, and sugar together three times. Beat egg yolks with vanilla till thick, and fold the dry ingredients into them. Beat egg whites till stiff and fold them into batter. Spread in pan. Bake 15 to 20 minutes and turn out on damp cloth. Remove paper, cut off hard edges, and roll up cake in cloth. When cake is cooled, unroll and spread with ice cream and roll up again. Slice and serve with hot chocolate sauce. Serves 12.

Sauce:

8 squares unsweetened chocolate
4 tablespoons butter
4 tablespoons white corn syrup
¾ cup sugar
1¾ cups milk
pinch salt

Melt chocolate with butter over hot water.
Add corn syrup, sugar and salt and blend.
Add milk and cook, stirring for 10 minutes.

*If you use chocolate ice cream you have
everything going for you on this one.*

CHOCOLATE FAR OUTS

Filling:

1 pint whipping cream
6 tablespoons sugar
4 tablespoons cocoa
1 teaspoon vanilla

Combine all ingredients, but do not beat.
Refrigerate for at least an hour.

Pastry:

1 cup water
¼ pound butter
½ teaspoon salt
1 cup sifted flour
4 eggs

Set oven at 375°. Lightly grease 2 cooky
sheets. In large saucepan combine water
with butter and salt. Heat over medium
heat till butter melts and water boils. Turn
heat low. Add flour all at once and beat
mixture vigorously till it leaves sides of
pan. Immediately remove from heat. With
wooden spoon, beat in eggs one at a time,
beating till smooth after each addition.
When eggs are blended, beat dough till
very smooth and satiny. Drop dough by
rounded tablespoonfuls onto cooky sheets,

about 2 inches apart, in rows 6 inches apart. Spread each ball into finger-length rectangles with rounded ends and smooth tops. Bake for 35 to 45 minutes or till lightly browned. Cool on rack. Cut thin layer off tops.

Beat filling till stiff and fill pastry shells. Replace tops.

Icing:

1 package (6 oz.) semi-sweet bits
2 tablespoons butter

Melt chocolate bits with butter over hot water till smooth. Spread over tops of pastries. Makes about 18.

You think they're ordinary cream puffs? No, these are far out.

CHOCOLATE SOMETHING ELSE

2 squares unsweetened chocolate
1 regular can sweetened condensed milk
6 large marshmallows
½ cup water
1 package (8¼ oz.) chocolate wafers
whipped cream

Melt chocolate in double boiler. Add milk and stir for 5 minutes till thickened. Add water and marshmallows and let marsh-mallows melt. Line 4¼" x 8¼" loaf pan with wax paper. Pour layer of chocolate mixture on bottom. Add layer of wafers. Repeat till all mixture is used. Top with layer of wafers. Refrigerate for 24 hours. Turn out on platter and carefully remove paper. Top with flavored whipped cream and sprinkle with sifted cocoa.

Remember the old recipes for icebox cake? Forget them, this is something else.

CHOCOLATE STUFF

1 pound sweet chocolate
1 teaspoon water
1 tablespoon flour
1 tablespoon sugar
¼ pound butter, softened
4 eggs, separated

Set oven at 425.° Grease an 8" spring-form pan. Melt chocolate with water over hot water. Remove from heat and stir in flour, sugar, and butter. Mix thoroughly. Beat egg yolks well, then stir into chocolate mixture gradually and smoothly. Beat egg whites till they hold a shape, and mix gently into the batter. Pour into pan and bake 15 to 20 minutes. Cool thoroughly, then chill. Serve in thin wedges with unsweetened whipped cream. Serves 6 to 8.

Neither pudding nor cake, but good for what ails you.

CHOCOLATE TRIP

Mousse:

1½ pounds semi-sweet chocolate
½ cup strong coffee
3 eggs, separated
½ cup cognac
¾ cup heavy cream
2 tablespoons sugar

Melt chocolate with coffee over low heat. Remove pot from flame and stir into melted chocolate the yolks, beaten till light. Gradually mix in cognac. Set mixture aside to cool. Whip cream. In separate bowl, beat whites. Gradually add sugar and beat till stiff. Fold whipped cream into the chocolate mixture, then the whites. Chill.

Cake:

4 eggs, separated
¼ cup sugar
½ teaspoon vanilla
½ cup sifted flour
½ cup sifted cornstarch

Set oven at 400°. Grease an 11 x 15″ jelly roll pan. Line with wax paper, grease and lightly flour. Beat whites till they form soft peaks. Add sugar, 1 tablespoon at a time, beating continuously till stiff and dry. Beat yolks slightly with a fork, stir in vanilla. Fold in one quarter (no more than that) of beaten whites, then pour this yolk mixture over the remaining whites. Sift flour and cornstarch together and then sift it again over the egg mixture. Fold in gently but thoroughly. Spread the cake batter evenly in the prepared pan. Bake for 10 minutes. Turn cake out onto rack, peel off the paper and allow to cool.

Lightly grease a 1½ quart pyrex bowl and line with the cake. Use a round of the cake for the bottom and a strip for the sides. Fill with the chilled mousse. Fit another round of the cake over the top. Chill for one hour. Unmold and cover with glaze.

Glaze:

½ pound semi-sweet chocolate
1/3 cup water

Melt chocolate in water and blend. Cover entire surface of molded dessert. Chill again. Serves 8 to 10.

Have a good trip.

CHOCOLATE STASH

¼ cup soft butter
2/3 cup sugar
1 cup sifted flour
1½ teaspoons baking powder
½ teaspoon salt
½ cup milk
1 square unsweetened chocolate, melted
1 teaspoon vanilla
¾ cup chopped nuts

2/3 cup sugar
½ cup brown sugar
3 tablespoons cocoa
¼ teaspoon salt
1½ cups boiling water
1 teaspoon vanilla

Set oven at 350°. Cream butter with sugar
till light. Sift flour with baking powder and
salt and add to butter mixture with milk,
stirring just enough to blend. Add melted
chocolate, vanilla and nuts. Spread batter
on bottom of 8" square pan. Combine sugar,
brown sugar, cocoa and salt. Sprinkle over
batter. Add vanilla to boiling water and
pour over top, but do not stir. Bake for 1
hour. (Sauce will be on the bottom, cake
on top). Cool slightly. Serve warm. Serves 9.

*Just as good cold...so put it in the fridge
for a rainy day.*

MISCELLANEOUS
JAZZ

CHOCOLATE LID

3 squares unsweetened chocolate
2 tablespoons butter
1/3 cup milk
1¼ cups sifted powdered sugar
1 teaspoon vanilla
1 egg

Dissolve chocolate in top of double boiler over hot water. Add butter and milk and mix. Remove from water and fill bottom of double boiler with ice cubes and cold water. Add sugar, vanilla, and egg to chocolate mixture and beat it for one minute at room temperature. Then put it over ice and beat with electric beater at high speed for about 15 minutes, till frosting is thick and light in color. Spread on completely cooled cake.

Cover any cake with this...it should be enough.

WILD CHOCOLATE

1 egg white
¾ cup sugar
2½ tablespoons cold water
pinch of salt
pinch of cream of tartar
1 teaspoon white karo syrup
1 teaspoon vanilla
1½ squares unsweetened chocolate, melted

Place all ingredients but vanilla and chocolate over rapidly boiling water. Beat constantly for about 6 minutes with electric beater till frosting will form peaks. Remove from heat. Add vanilla. Beat till cooled. After spreading on cake, drip melted chocolate over top and swirl into frosting with knife.

A bittersweet frosting that's really wild!

MOST CHOCOLATE

1 cup light cream
1 cup sugar
1 cup Ghiradelli's ground chocolate
pinch of salt
1/3 stick butter
1 teaspoon vanilla

Mix all ingredients except butter and vanilla
in a heavy pot. Boil slowly for about 45
minutes, or to the soft-ball stage. Take off
fire and add butter and vanilla. Set aside
to cool for a few minutes. Beat. Spread
on cake.

A chocolate fudge frosting to cry from!

CHOCOLATE TEA

1 pound milk chocolate
2 cups light cream
2 tablespoons creme de cacao
½ cup coarsely chopped toasted almonds

Over low heat melt chocolate in cream.
Bring mixture to rolling boil, stirring constantly. Turn down the heat and simmer
till it thickens. Add flavoring and nuts.

*Feeling low? Make a pitcher of this and
pour it over something...anything.*

CHOCOLATE HIGH

1 cup Ghiradelli's ground chocolate
2 cups powdered sugar
1 cup heavy cream
1 cup water
1 teaspoon vanilla

Mix chocolate and sugar together in top of
double boiler. Scald cream and water.
Place chocolate and sugar over boiling water.
Add scalded liquid slowly. Stir well, then
cook for half an hour. Add vanilla. Pour
into pyrex jar. Refrigerate when cool.

*Good thing to keep handy in the fridge. Drink
it right out of the jar when nobody's looking.*

CHOCOLATE FLIPS

1 package (6 oz.) semi-sweet chocolate bits
3 tablespoons corn syrup
½ cup bourbon
½ pound vanilla wafers, crushed
½ cup powdered sugar
1 cup chopped nuts

Melt chocolate over hot water. Add corn syrup and bourbon. Combine crumbs, sugar, nuts. Add to chocolate mixture. Drop by small amounts in powdered sugar and roll into balls. Let stand in refrigerator for a couple of hours. Roll in powdered sugar again.

A nice thing to keep around. Pop one in your mouth when things get rough.

CHOCOLATE DIGS

1 pound large soft dried figs
¼ cup heavy cream
2 ounces sweet chocolate
½ teaspoon dark rum
2 ounces sweet chocolate
½ pint sour cream
cinnamon

Slit the figs and widen a pocket in each
with the thumbs. Heat the cream and
2 ounces of chocolate together over
hot water till chocolate is melted. Then
put over direct heat and let the mixture boil up once, stirring constantly.
Remove the mixture from the heat and
stir over a bowl of ice till cold. Add
rum. Fill the figs with the mixture
(about ½ teaspoon in each). Chill.
Melt the 2 ounces sweet chocolate over
hot water. Remove figs from refrigerator and press the slits closed. Dip into
melted chocolate and coat them halfway.
Dry on wax paper. Chill thoroughly.
Serve with sour cream with cinnamon
to taste.

*Kind of an odd combination, but groovy,
you dig?*

CHOCOLATE COOLS

1 package (6 oz.) semi-sweet chocolate bits
1 pint chocolate mocha ice cream, slightly
   softened

Melt chocolate bits in top of double boiler
over hot water. Using a pastry brush,
spread evenly on bottom and almost to
tops of sides of 12 paper nut cups placed
in a muffin tin. Freeze till hardened.
Carefully peel off paper and freeze again.
Taking one at a time, fill each cup with
ice cream. Return to freezer, covered,
till ready to serve.

Nothing quite so cool!

CHOCOLATE TURN ONS

1 small can dark pitted cherries, drained
3 tablespoons brandy
1 quart chocolate ice cream
chocolate shot

Pour brandy over cherries and refrigerate
for 24 hours, drain. Fill large ice-cream
scoop half-full with ice cream. Place 2
cherries in the center. Cover with rest
of ice cream to form a ball. Unmold on
cooky sheet. Repeat to make 8 balls.
Sprinkle with chocolate shot. Freeze.
When frozen, cover till ready to serve.

*Now isn't that a nice little surprise to find
inside a ball of chocolate?*

CHOCOLATE OHZEE

2 tablespoons butter
2 tablespoons cocoa
2 tablespoons sugar
2 tablespoons milk
scant teaspoon vanilla

Melt, stirring constantly, butter, cocoa, and sugar. Remove from heat. Add milk, vanilla. Blend thoroughly and return to fire, stirring constantly, till thick and shiny, about 1 minute. Serves 1.

When you're strung out and haven't time to really cook, throw this together, it works!